AF304744

MAN UNRAVELING

. . . .

Alice Wong

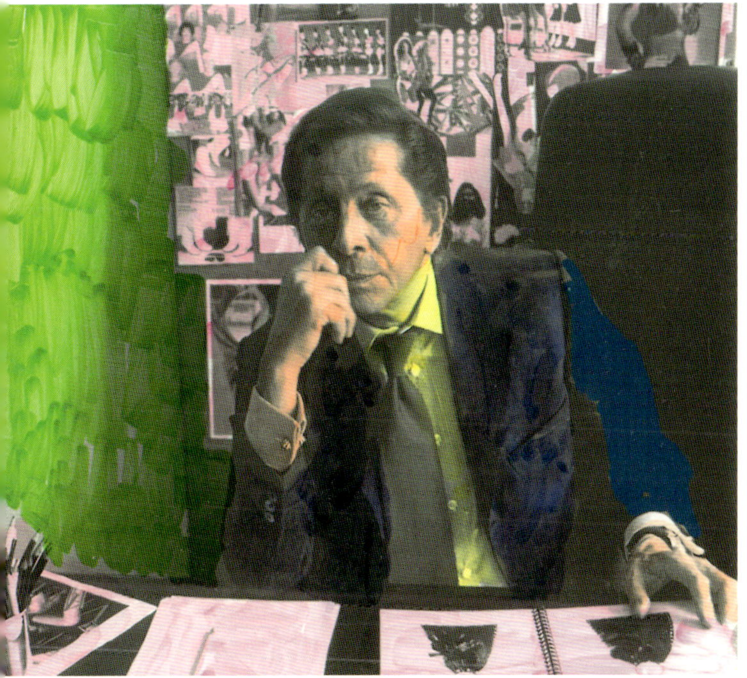

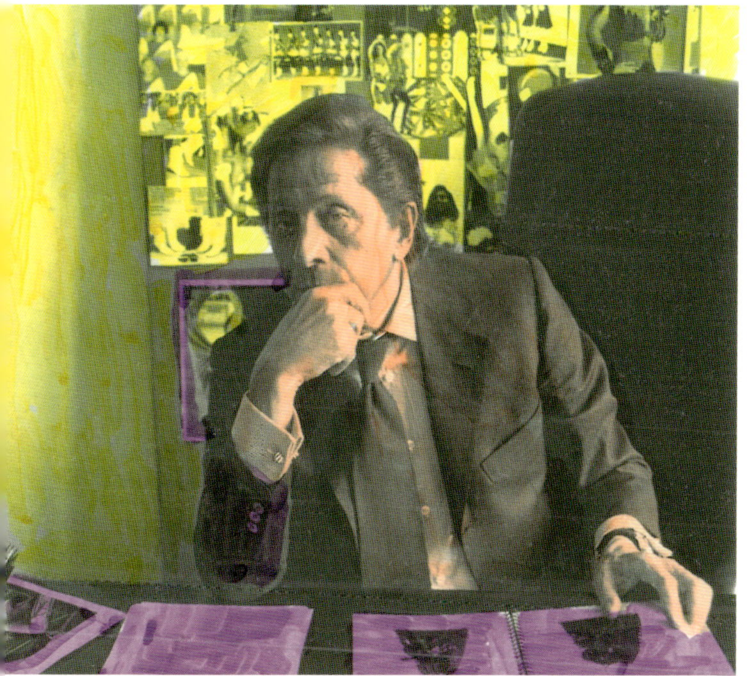

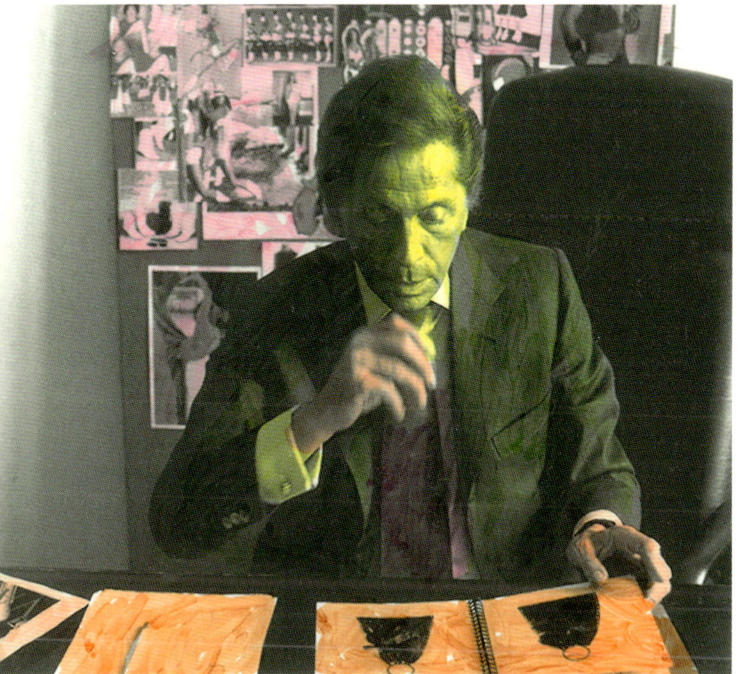

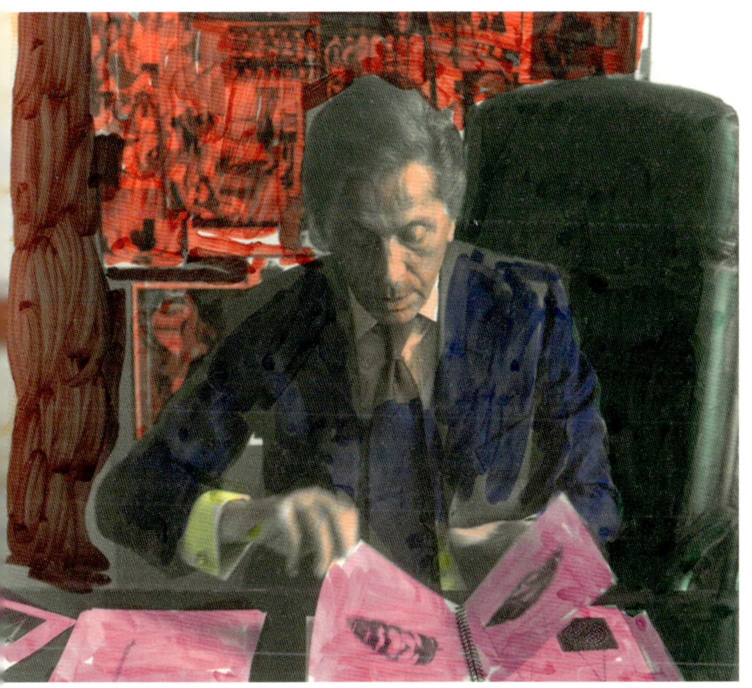

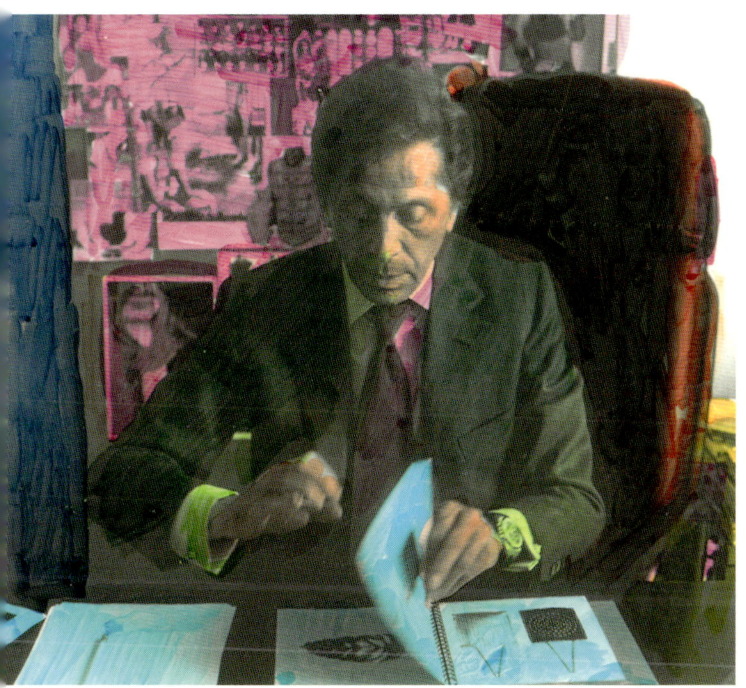

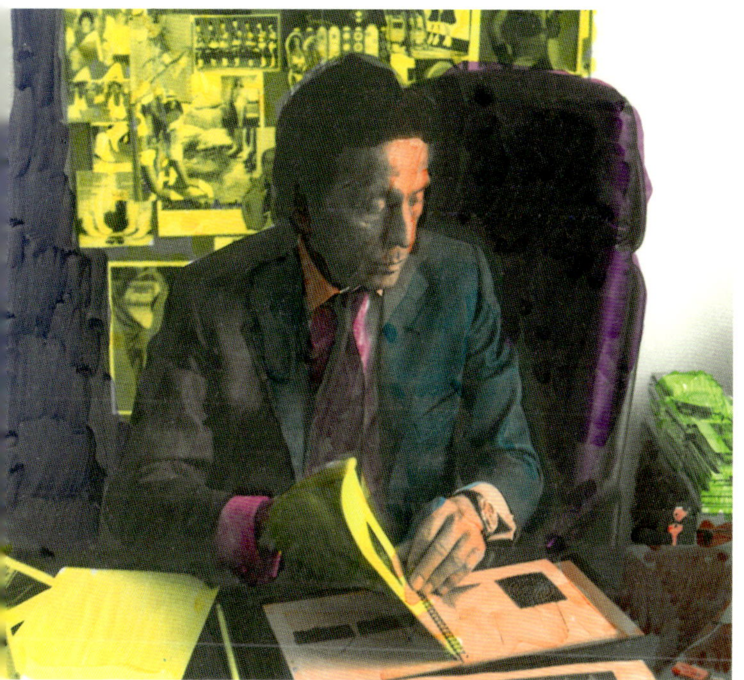

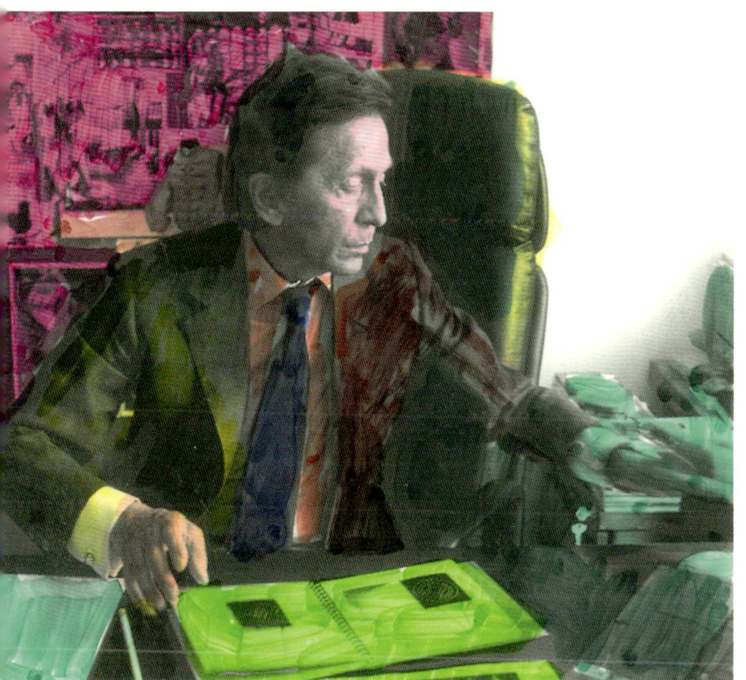

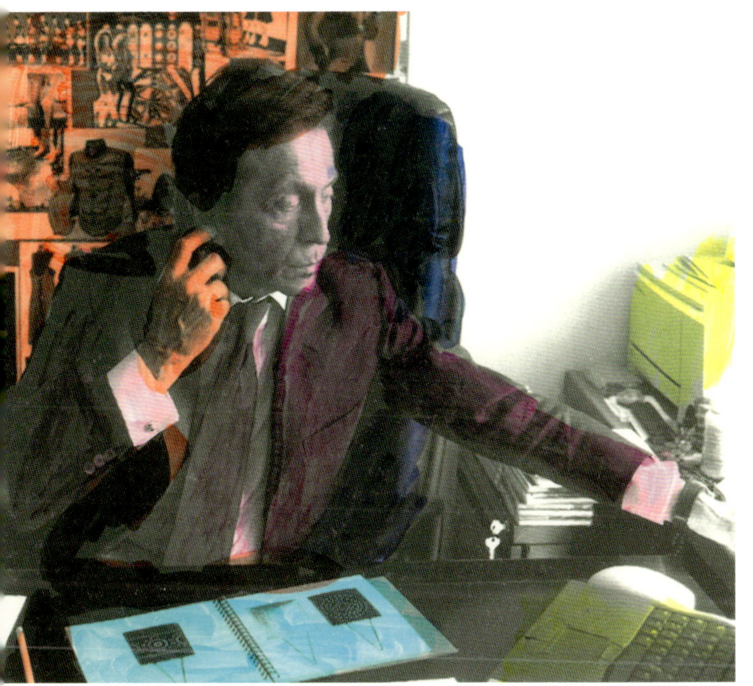

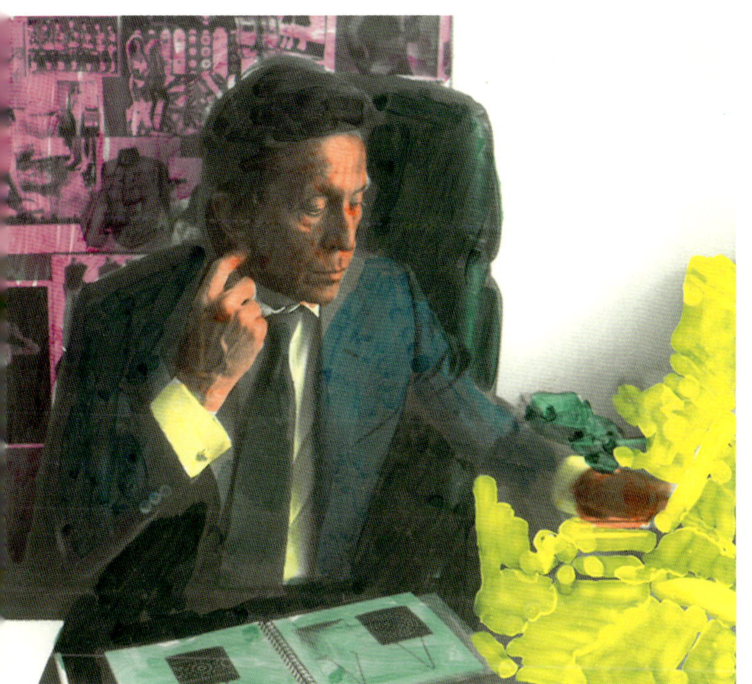

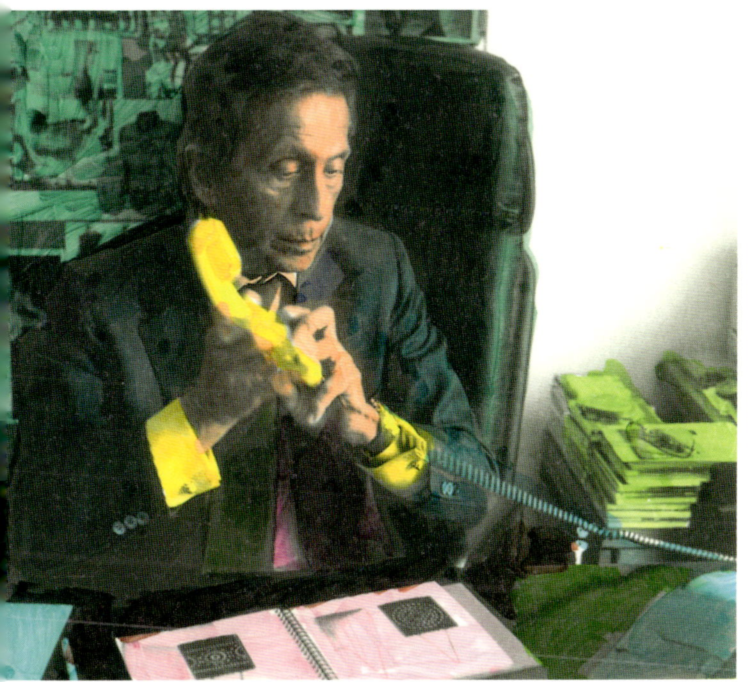

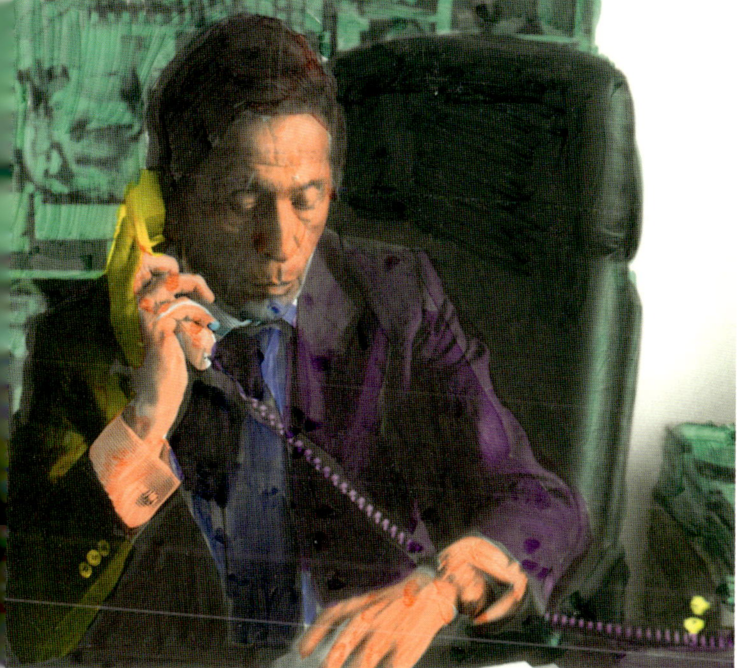

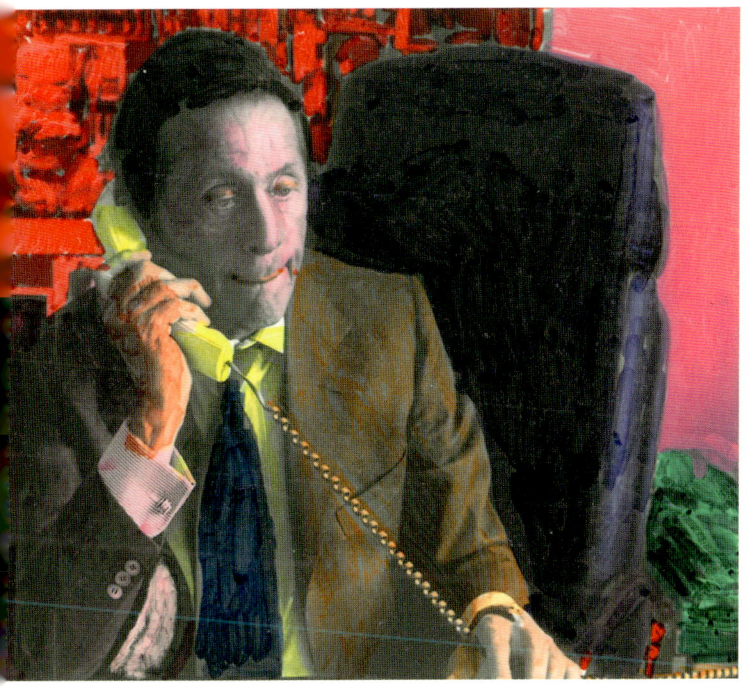

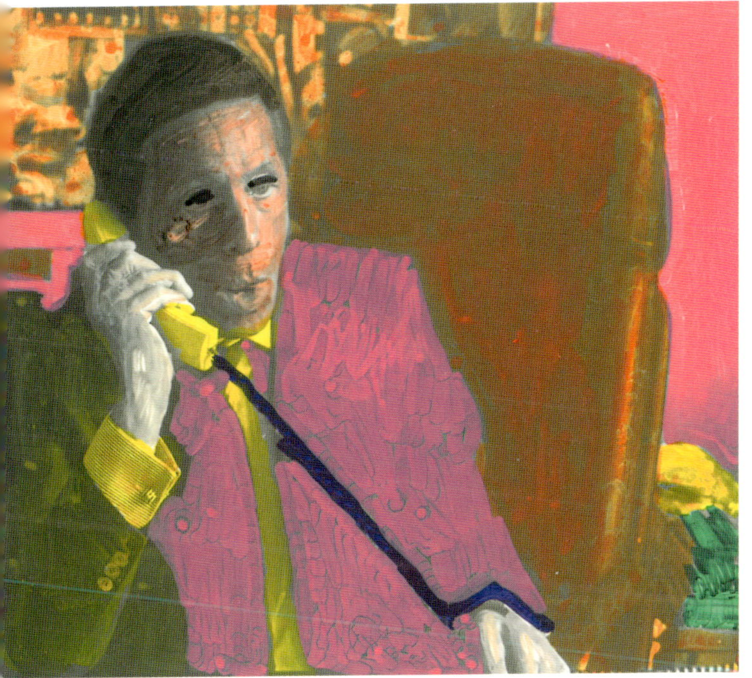

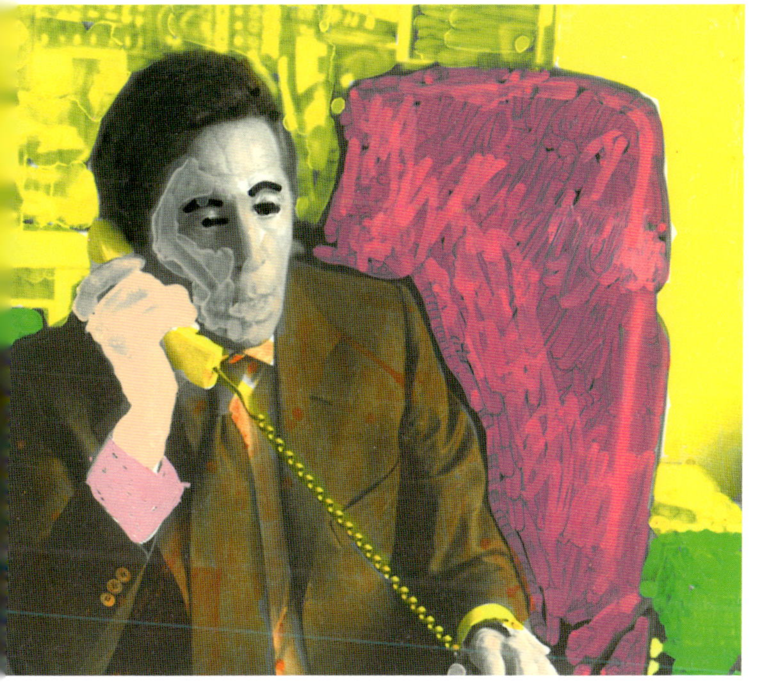

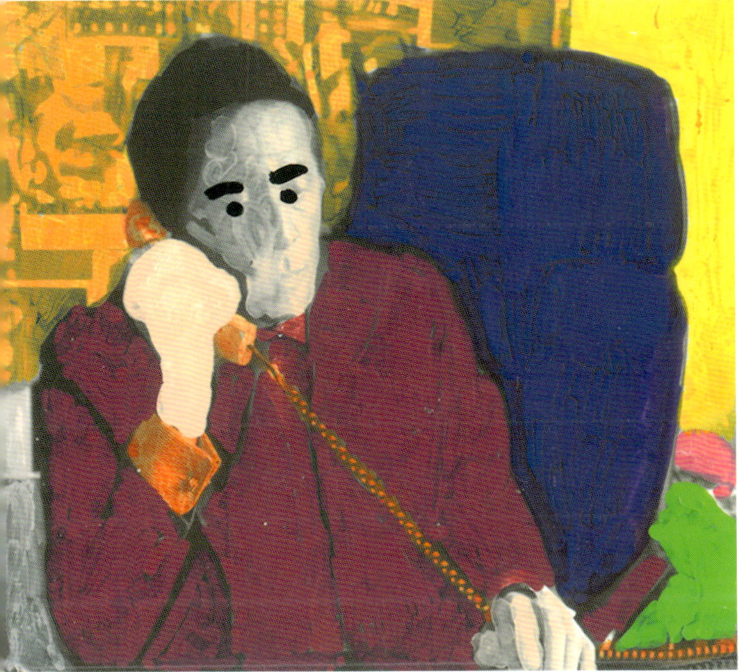

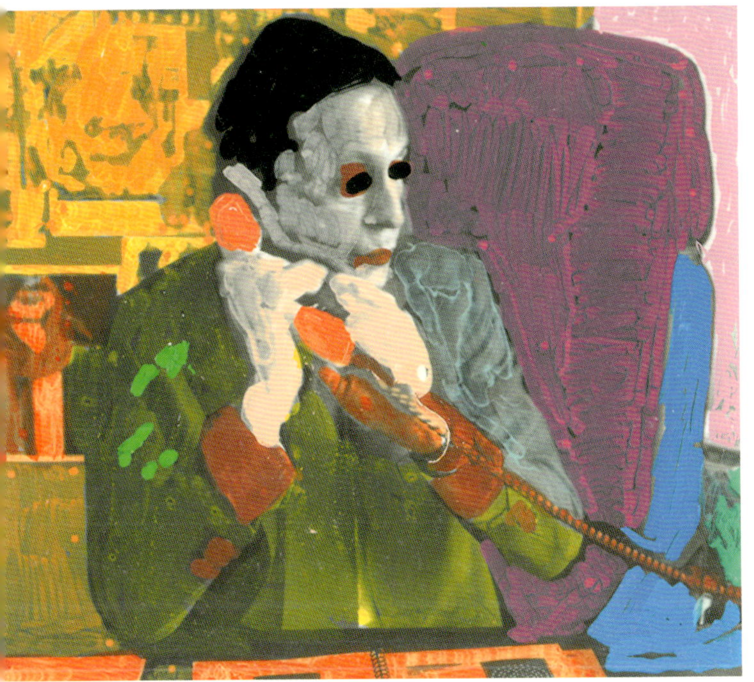

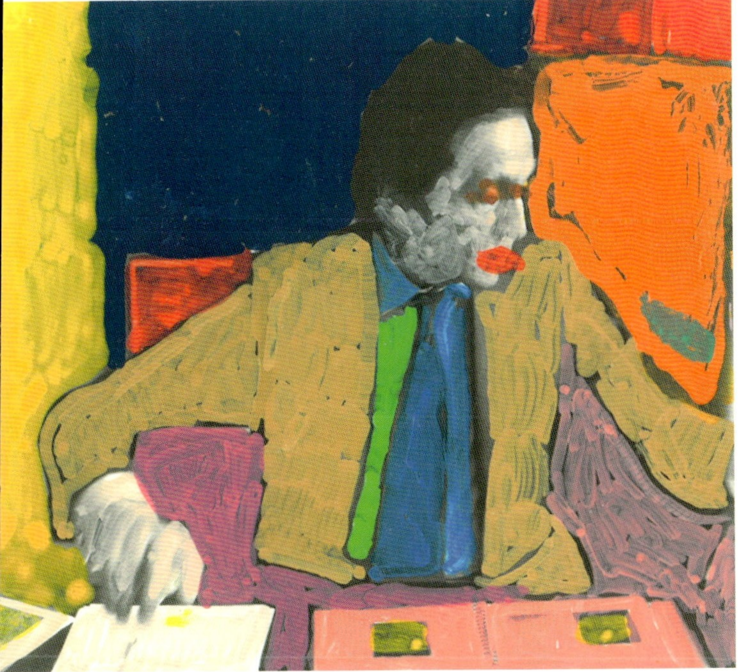

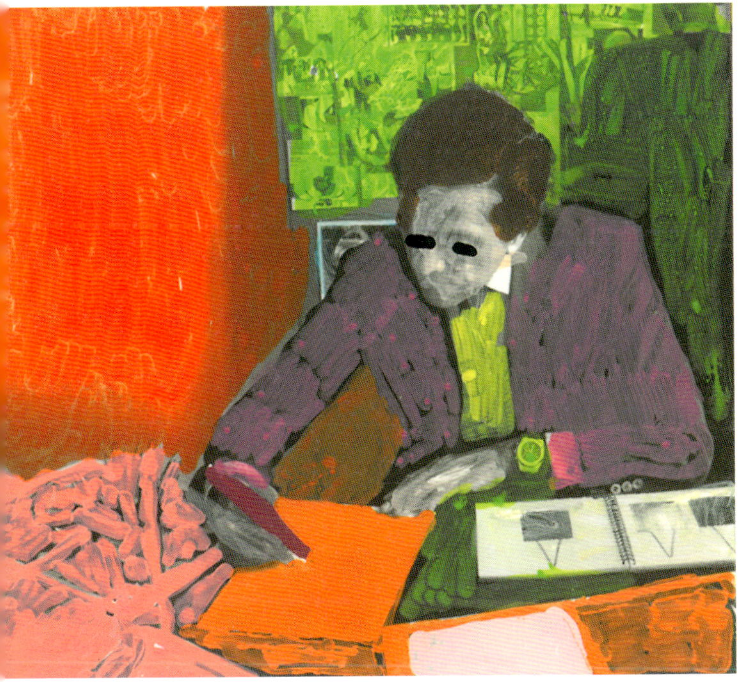

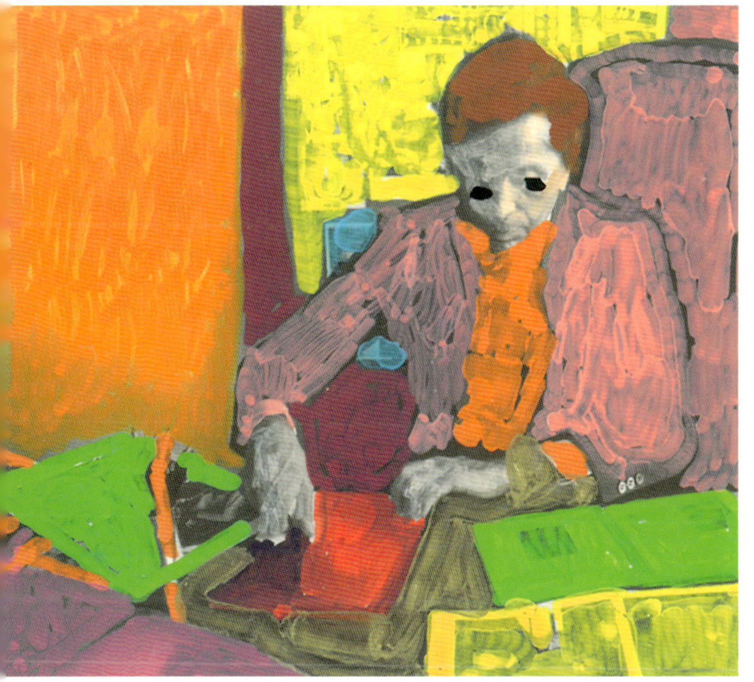

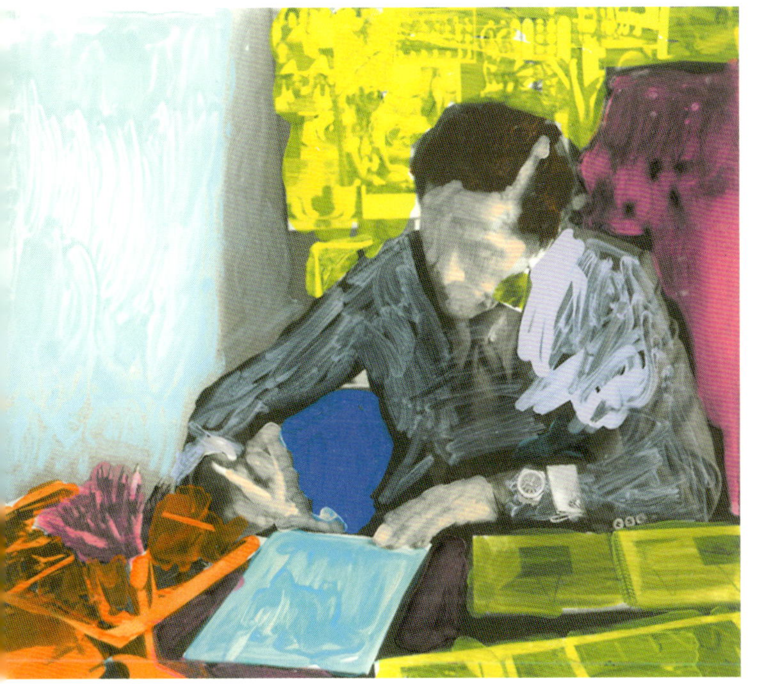

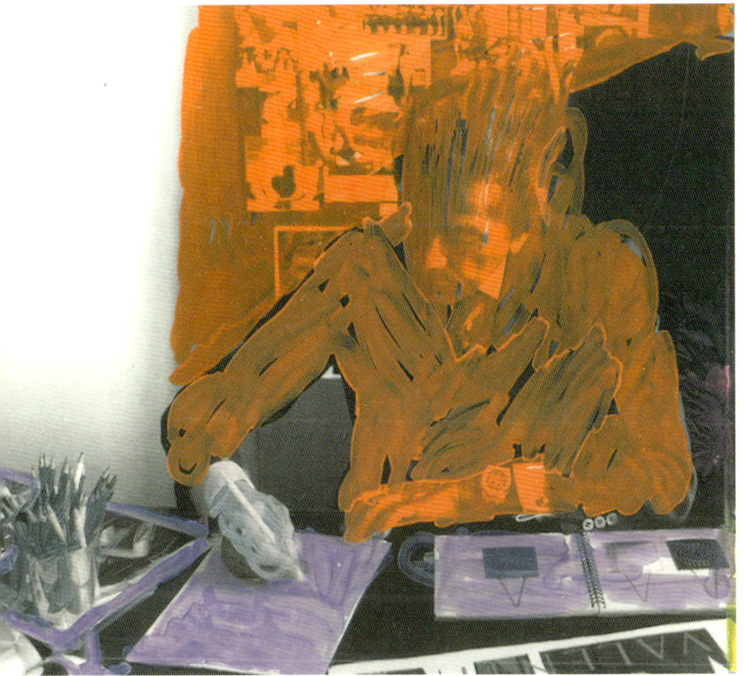

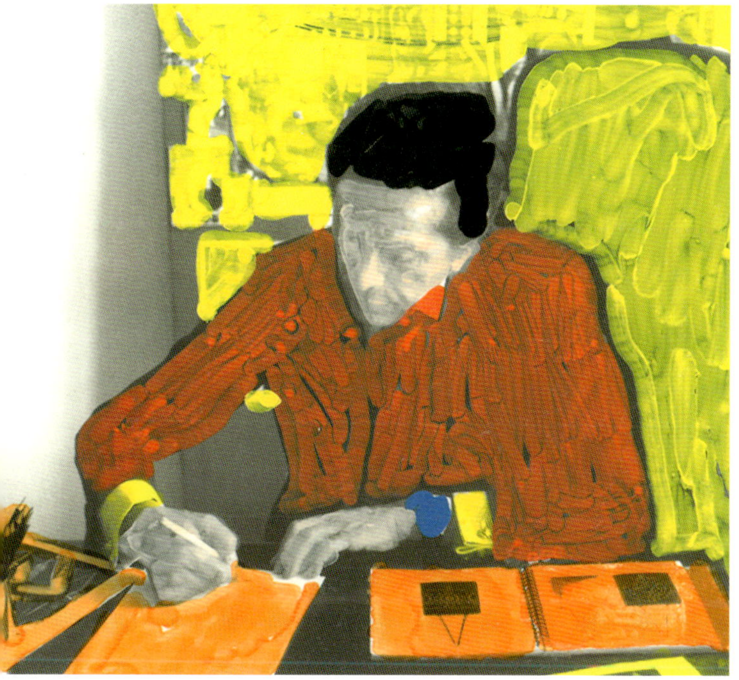

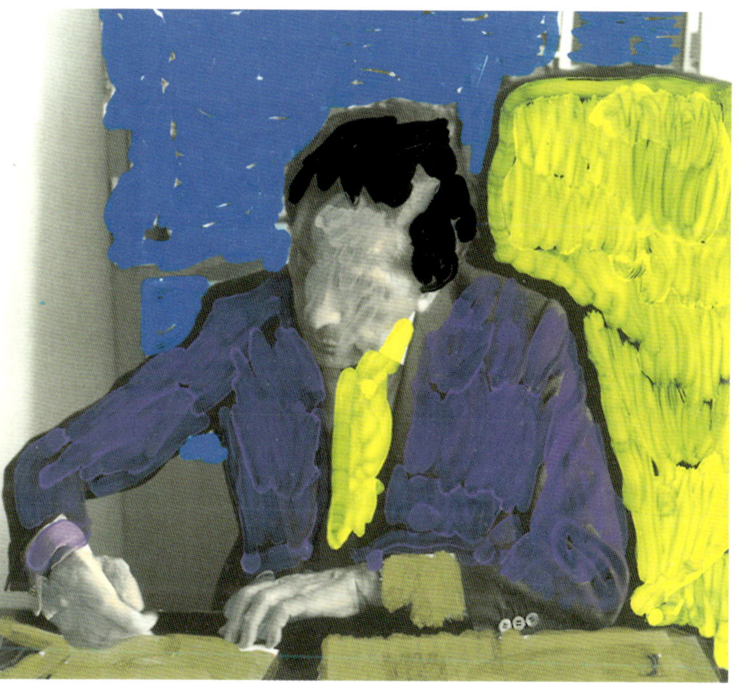

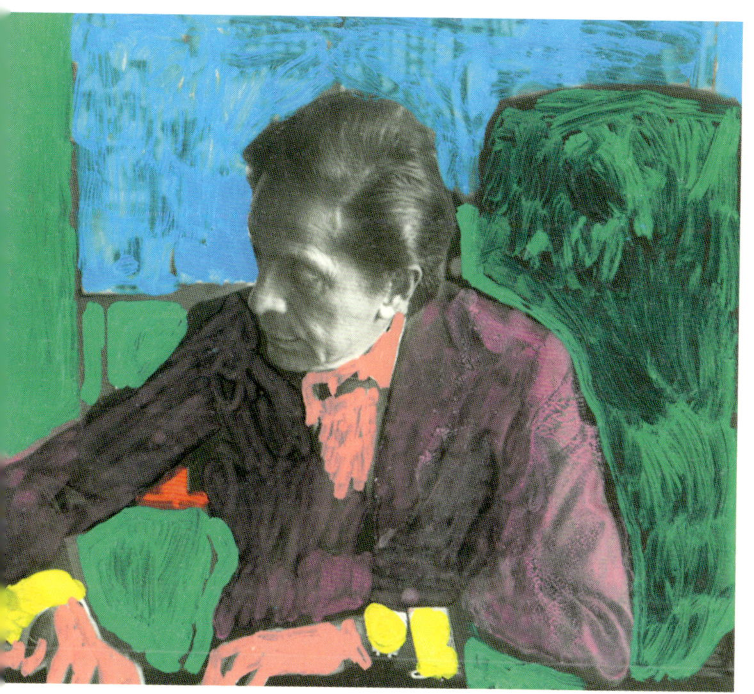

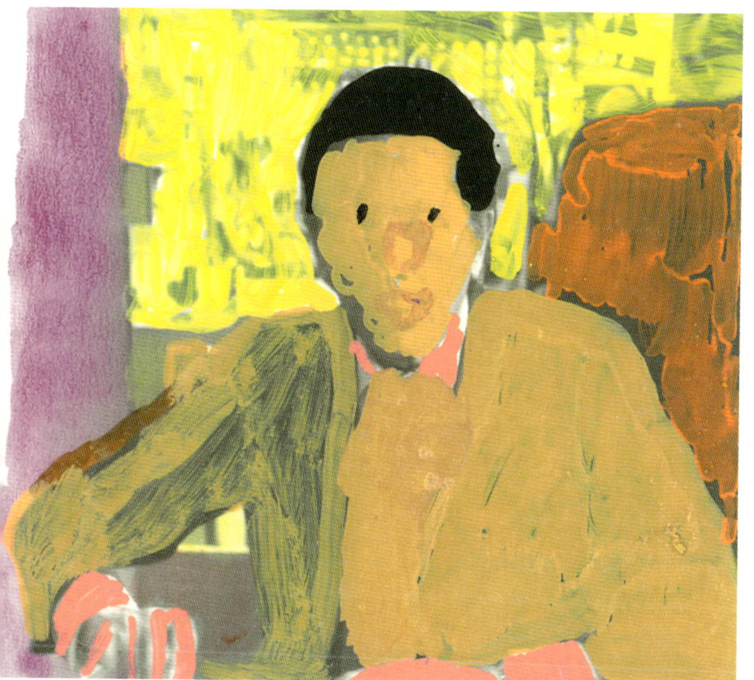

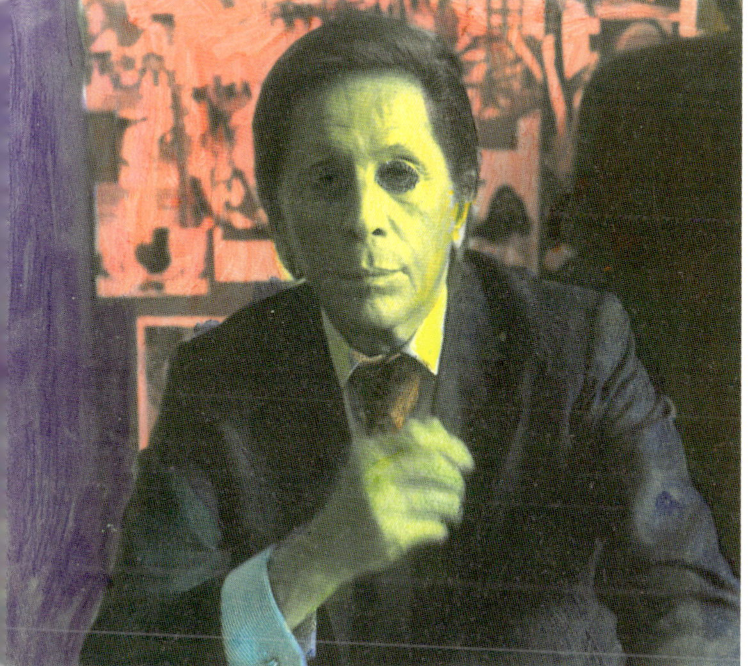

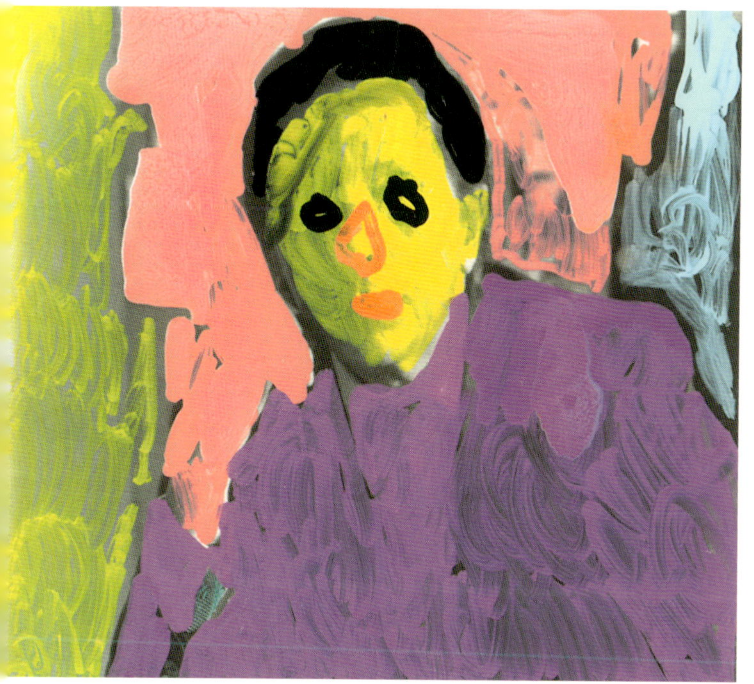

Alice Wong was born in Hong Kong in 1980 and began working in Creative Growth's studio in 2003, when she moved to California with her family.

Creative Growth Art Center is the oldest and largest nonprofit art studio for artists with developmental disabilities. Since 1974, Creative Growth has played a significant role in increasing public interest in the artistic capabilities and achievements of people with disabilities, providing a professional studio environment for artistic development, gallery exhibition, and representation.

TBW Books is an independent photobook publishing house in Oakland, California, since 2006(ish).

Art and books are in Oakland.

• •

www.creativegrowth.org
www.tbwbooks.com

This edition © TBW Books, 2022 · All images © Alice Wong, 2022 · ISBN 978-1-942953-55-5